GERMANY

A PICTURE BOOK TO REMEMBER HER BY

Designed by
DAVID GIBBON

Produced by
TED SMART

CRESCENT

INTRODUCTION

The Federal Republic of West Germany was formed after the Second World War from the three western zones of Germany then occupied by France, America and Britain, which split from the eastern sector, occupied by the USSR. The former capital, Berlin, though completely surrounded by Soviet-dominated East Germany, was divided too and in 1949 Bonn became the capital and seat of the new German Parliament. Berlin, despite its history, is a vital and stimulating city and after nearly thirty years it still remains the capital in the hearts and emotions of many Germans.

Politically and geographically the Federal Republic is made up of the following regions, or *Länder,* each of which sends delegates to the Upper House of Parliament: Schleswig Holstein and Lower Saxony, which lie within the vast German-Polish northern plateau and consequently have a predominantly flat landscape; North Rhine Westphalia and Hesse, commonly called the *Mittelgebirge* – the land of the medium-sized mountains; Saarland, the main industrial area; the Rhineland-Palatinate, a romantic region of ancient castles and terraced vineyards; Baden-Württemberg, the home of the Black Forest with its many spas and health resorts; and Bavaria, the largest of the *Länder* and the main holiday region of Germany.

Since the Second World War, Germany has emerged as one of the most prosperous and technologically advanced countries in Europe, a fact that can be attributed, at least in part, to the hard work and conscientiousness of her people. Industry is booming and major exports include electrical equipment, chemicals, motor vehicles and textiles. Coal is mined from the large coalfields of the Ruhr and the Saar and shipbuilding is another important industry.

Hard work, though, is only part of the German way of life. Culturally, her greatest contribution has been in the field of music, and the list of German composers is a remarkable one: Bach, Beethoven, Brahms, Handel, Richard Strauss, Wagner and many more. The Germans appreciate their musical heritage; there are 97 state and city theatres and opera houses which all perform opera regularly to well-attended houses. German literature reached its peak at the turn of the 18th century with the works of such men as Goethe and Schiller, and philosophers such as Kant, Hegel, Schopenhauer and Nietzsche have all had a tremendous impact on world thought.

Wherever the visitor to Germany goes he will be aware of the wealth of stories and legends that are attached to the places around him, from the Pied Piper in Hamelin and Till Eulenspiegel in Brunswick to the Lorelei on the Rhine and the Witches of Brocken in the Harz Mountains. Legends and stories are tremendously important in the German way of life, and, apart from the tales of the Brothers Grimm, perhaps the best known and best loved is the story of the Ring of the Nibelungen, which provided the inspiration for Richard Wagner's great operatic cycle.

If the visitor is conscious of the legends of the places he sees then he must also be aware of the influence of history upon them. In the Rhineland, for instance, nearly every castle is either ruined or has had to be restored or rebuilt as a result of the destruction caused by the Thirty Years War and the Orleans War a few years later. The Thirty Years War which started in 1618 was a mainly religious conflict and caused Germany to become the battlefield of Europe, ravaging nearly the whole country. The Orleans War took place after the Elector Palatine, Karl Ludwig, married his daughter to Philip of Orleans, brother of Louis XIV, in the hope of ensuring peace in the Rhineland. In 1685, Karl Ludwig died without heir and Louis claimed the Rhineland territories under the terms of the marriage treaty. The resulting war devastated the area and destroyed many Rhineland castles as well as the entire towns of Heidelberg and Mannheim. The bombing of the Second World War has had a more recent and equally damaging effect upon the face of Germany.

The German *hausfrau* was once a traditional figure, with her preoccupation with the three K's – *Kinde* (children), *Küche* (cooking) and *Kirche* (church) and while German women have become liberated along with their European sisters it is certainly true that many are excellent cooks and German food is always wholesome and plentiful. A local speciality is the sausage *(Wurst)* which varies from region to region and comes in all sizes. Perhaps the most well-known are the Bratwurst of Nuremberg and the Frankfurter.

Many people think of Germany as the beer centre of the world, and the beer centre of Germany is Munich. Every year a huge festival is held there, called the Oktoberfest, and enormous beer halls are erected and brass bands play. Beer is drunk from mugs which hold a litre, the only measure allowed on the grounds.

Germany's other national drink is her wine, which comes from two main areas, the Rhine and the Mosel. These two are the most northerly vineyards of any importance in the world, and it is surprising that they are also the most ancient, dating back to Roman times. Queen Victoria was especially fond of Rhine wines and obtained her supply from vineyards at Hochheim near Mainz, which is how in England Rhine wine came to be known as hock. Germany now exports much of her wine and it is justly famous throughout the world.

Left: Darmstadt

At the heart of modern Berlin is the Kaiser Wilhelm Memorial Church in the Kurfürstendamm *above*. The old church, with its broken tower, has been kept as a reminder of the destruction of war and is incorporated into a group of modern buildings which include the new church and a campanile.

Completely restored after World War II, the Reichstag *middle right* is the old House of Parliament where meetings of the Imperial Diet were held. Assemblies and conferences are held in the Kongresshalle *right*, which irreverent Berliners refer to as "the pregnant oyster".

The Victory Column *far right* commemorates the Prussian successes against Austria and France in the 1860s. The observation platform at the top provides magnificent views over East Berlin.

Schleswig Holstein is the most northern of the German Länder and lies within the great northern plain. The country is consequently predominantly flat but the scenery is varied and the visitor will find beaches, forests and fiords as well as heaths and moorland.

The decorated barn doors *left* are in a village near Katharinenheerd in the Eiserstedt region.

Concerts are held in the moated castle at Glücksberg *right* which is situated at the northern tip of Schleswig Holstein.

Travemünde is on the Baltic coast at the mouth of the River Trave and is a popular resort with its casino and pleasure harbour *below left*. The Holstentor in nearby Lübeck *below* is now a museum but was built in 1477 as a rather imposing gateway in the subsequent perimeter wall of the town.

Friedrichstadt *below right* lies on the River Eider on the North Sea coast.

Hamburg is one of the largest ports in Europe and is Germany's second city after Berlin. The port *above* consists of 60 dock basins with 58 kilometres of quays and it handles 800 departures a month.

In the centre of the city is Lake Alster *below left*, a beautiful expanse of water surrounded by luxurious houses and pleasure gardens. From the middle of the lake the "Michel" can be seen *above left*, the famous tower of St. Michaelis Church and the town's popular symbol.

Like most large ports Hamburg has a thriving nightlife and the Reeperbahn *left* is famous throughout the world.

Brunswick is a prosperous town in the middle of the "Lower Saxony Vegetable Garden". It was chosen as the permanent residence in the twelfth century of Henry the Lion, Duke of Bavaria, and is rich in historic buildings, such as the Guild House and Workshop *above*.

Hannoversch Münden *top* is situated on the confluence of the rivers Fulda and Werra. In the old city centre there are more than 450 half-timbered houses built in a variety of styles.

The Romanesque Church of St. Michael in Hildesheim *left* dates from the 11th century and has been rebuilt since 1945.

The Harz Mountains, which have been called the Heart of Germany, cover an area of 2,000 square kms. and are a popular resort in both summer and winter. Mount Brocken, scene of Walpurgisnacht (the Witches' Sabbath), lies just over the border in East Germany.

Ernst August of Hanover, father of George I of England, was born in the 900 year old Schloss Herzberg *right* on the southern edge of the Harz.

The Sieber Valley *above* is typical of the great natural beauty of the region.

Covered in a mantle of snow, this Nordic Stave Church *left* is in Hahnenklee in the Upper Harz.

Overleaf: Cologne Cathedral and the Hohenzollern Railway Bridge.

In 1949, Bonn *above*, then a quiet university town, was chosen to be the seat of the new federal government. Since then the population has increased enormously and many new buildings now rub shoulders with those of a more traditional kind, such as the rococo Town Hall *left*.

Surrounded by cherry trees, the Schwanenburg in Kleve *right* was the birthplace of Anne of Cleves, the fourth wife of Henry VIII. It is also associated with the legend of Lohengrin.

The valley of the River Mosel *above* is famous for its light dry white wines. Vineyards cling to even the steepest of the valley sides and little wine-growing villages such as Beilstein *above left,* lying at the foot of the ruined Metternich castle, and Bremm *below* cluster along its banks.

The castle at Cochem *below left* was destroyed in the Orleans War in 1689, only the base of the walls and the keep remaining. However, in the 19th century it was completely rebuilt in 14th century style.

The village of Monschau *above left* is in the area known as the Eifel which lies to the west of the stretch of the Rhine running between Bonn and Koblenz. Although geographically the Eifel is a plateau, the scenery is varied, with forests of beech and spruce, rushing rivers, valleys and wooded hills.

Schloss Bürresheim *above* lies in the valley of the River Nette in the Upper Eifel. It was built as a fortress in the 12th century and then a baroque chateau was added to it in the 17th century. It is now a museum.

Pilgrims and worshippers have visited the Benedictine Abbey of Maria Laach *below left* for centuries. This 12th century monastery is magnificently situated on the edge of a volcanic lake called the Laach, hence its name.

Koblenz *left* stands on the confluence of the Mosel
and the Rhine and gets its name from the Latin
"confluentia". It marks the beginning of the
spectacular 65 kilometres of river known as the
Rhine Gorge.

Like the Mosel valley, the Rhinelands are
renowned for their fine wines and Oppenheim *above*
is one of the three greatest names among German
wine towns.

The most picturesque part of that historic highway, the Rhine, is the stretch between Koblenz and Bingen. There are about 30 castles in this area alone, most of them built in the Middle Ages when the Rhineland was at its wealthiest, and every one has its own story to tell. One of these is the Marksburg *below right* which was built to protect the silver and lead mining interests in the town of Braubach. It is the only castle on the Rhine never to have been destroyed and it is now administered by the association for the preservation of German castles.

The ruins of Gutenfels Castle *above right* lie above Castle Pfalz which was erected by Ludwig of Bavaria to extort customs dues. Burg Katz *above* is named after its builders, the counts of Katzenelnbogen. It was blown up by the French in 1804 because, according to one story, a salvo fired in Napoleon's honour made his horse shy.

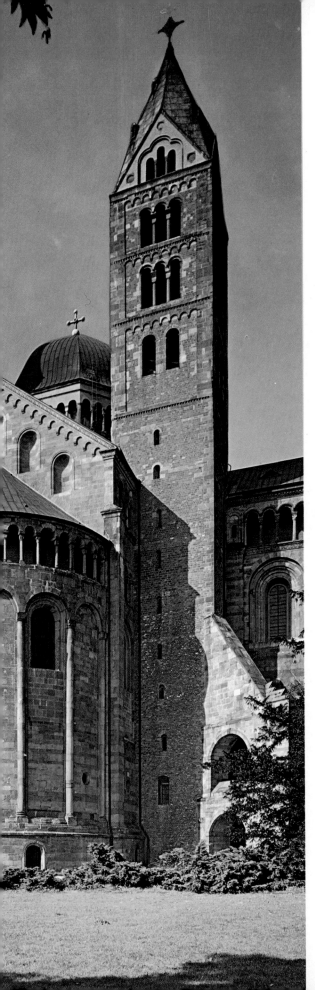

Speyer Cathedral *left* and the west chancel of St. Peter's Cathedral in Worms *far left* are two of the best examples of Rhineland Romanesque architecture in Germany. One of the characteristics of this style is the dwarf gallery which runs round the nave and transept just below the roof.

St. Castor's Church in Koblenz *above* stands on the site of an earlier basilica where the Treaty of Verdun was drawn up sharing Charlemagne's empire between his three grandsons.

The sandstone hills and magnificent forests of the Odenwald *above left* lie to the east of the Rhine and to the north of Heidelberg and were the hunting grounds of the legendary Nibelungen. Michelstadt *far left* is known as the heart of the Odenwald and attracts many visitors with its half-timbered houses and fairy-tale town hall.

Spangenberg Castle, which has now been converted into a hotel and restaurant, lies on the outskirts of Kassel, the capital city of Hesse. In Kassel itself is the Wilhelmshöhe Park, which extends across the slopes of the Habichtswald and was commissioned by the Landgrave Karl of Hesse in 1701. The Apollo Temple *left* is only one of the many temples, follies and statues that can be found in the gardens.

Overleaf: The castle and city of Heidelberg.

Heidelberg is perhaps the city that most of all sums up romantic Germany. The old town *below*, rebuilt since a catastrophic fire in 1693, clusters at the foot of the Church of the Holy Spirit and contains the oldest university in Germany. The Old Bridge *left* over the River Neckar is not quite as old as its name suggests; it was destroyed in the war and rebuilt afterwards.

The Castle *right* is the focal point of Heidelberg. Originally built in the fourteenth century as the residence of the Prince-Electors of the Palatinate, it was repeatedly added to in a variety of styles; Gothic, Renaissance and Baroque. It was blown up in the Orleans War and although it is now a ruin much remains to be seen of these architectural differences.

Laufen is the German for rapids and at Laufenberg-am-Rhein *above left*, in Baden-Württemberg, the river runs across hard limestone which causes them.

The picturesque tannery *above* is in the village of Ortenau near Gengenbach.

The castle of Schwetzingen *left* was rebuilt after having been another casualty of the Orleans War, and became the summer palace of the Palatine Electors when they abandoned Heidelberg.

The Friedrichplatz *far left* is in Mannheim, where the Electors had their winter residence.

The Black Forest *right and top left overleaf* may have its dark and sinister side, typified perhaps by such places as the Witch Hole *above*, but as there is a continuous contrast between open countryside and pine woods it is neither black, nor entirely forest.

The wooden sign near Schiltach *left* reflects the craftsmanship that has resulted in the cuckoo clock becoming the Black Forest symbol.

Wolfach *left and top right* is one of the many attractive villages that have helped to make the Black Forest one of the most popular holiday centres in Germany.

Freiburg am Breisgau is the capital of the region and the cathedral *right* is particularly known for the beauty and delicacy of its Gothic spire.

Munich is the capital of Bavaria, the
third largest city in Germany and a
noted artistic and cultural centre.
The life of the town is concentrated
in the Marienplatz *above* on one
side of which is the New Town Hall
with its famous Glockenspiel; at
eleven o'clock every morning
enamelled copper figures emerge
and go through the ritual of a
miniature tournament.

Other sights to be seen in Munich city centre include the Residenz *left*, the former palace of the Dukes of Wittelsbach, which now houses one of Munich's excellent museums, and the Teatiner Church, seen *right* from the Hofgarten.

Munich was the home of the ill-fated 20th Olympics in 1972 and the stadium with its famous tent-like roof in Olympia Park *left* is still used for national and international football matches. Also outside the city is the famous Nymphenburg castle and park *right*, originally the summer residence of the Bavarian kings and now a popular spot not only with tourists but also with the inhabitants of Munich.

Every year Munich celebrates the Oktoberfest, a festival of beer drinking which has taken place regularly since 1810 and lasts for sixteen days. Enormous beer tents are erected on the Theresienwiese *below* and every day two oxen are roasted on a spit.

Overleaf: The village of Wasserburg on Lake Constance.

Nuremberg is architecturally one of the most richly endowed
cities in Germany and although it suffered much damage in the
war many ancient buildings still stand, such as the Hospital of the
Holy Ghost *above* which was founded in 1331 and is now used as a
wine cellar. Nuremberg's most famous inhabitant was Albrecht
Dürer and the house in which he lived until his death in 1528 *right*
is now a museum with exhibitions of original drawings and copies
of his important works.

One of Nuremberg's best known sights is the 14th century Gothic Schöner Brunnen, or Beautiful Fountain *right*. The figures round the base are the seven Electors and nine heroes of the Old Testament and the Middle Ages; those at the top are the Prophets round Moses.

A few miles to the east of Nuremberg is the beautiful old town of Amberg *above right*.

The unfortunate Ludwig II of Bavaria spent his childhood in Hohenschwangau Castle *below* and years later he could see from its windows the building work in progress of his new castle at Neuschwanstein across the valley *left*. The original plans of this fairy-tale palace were drawn up not by an architect but by a theatrical director and the interior is just as dreamlike as the outside.

The Lindenhof *right* was also built by Ludwig II, but not to such extravagant specifications. However, in the park can be found, among other things, a copy of the Blue Grotto in Capri, and a Turkish salon where majolica vases and enamelled peacocks are on display.

The Romantic Road, which was opened in 1950, covers the 350 kilometres between Würzburg and Füssen and provides, as the guide books say, the concentrated essence of picturebook Germany. Near Würzburg at the northern end is Aschaffenburg with its huge Renaissance palace *left*. Forty kilometres to the south lies Miltenberg *below*, a small town well-known for its most unusual half-timbered houses. The road travels on for a hundred kilometres of wild landscape, castle ruins and attractive villages until it reaches Rothenburg ob der Tauber *right* where the visitor is immediately plunged into the 16th century atmosphere. Rothenburg is the best preserved example of a medieval town in Germany; all the ramparts, gates and towers are still intact.

The moated castle of Messelbrünn *above* lies at the northern end of the Romantic Road near Aschaffenburg.

To the north of Rothenburg stands Weikersheim Castle with its magnificent Knights' Hall *far right*. The ceiling is painted with hunting themes; the monumental doorway is decorated with sculptured figures of emperors and empresses.

After Rothenburg the road passes through the sleepy town of Dinklesbühl *right and top right*, another example of a well-preserved medieval town, with moats, bastions, gates and towers all standing.

Next on the road is Donauwörth which lies on a hillside running steeply down to the Danube and is dominated by the Church of the Holy Cross *top left*.

The Romantic Road continues southwards through the medieval town of Landsberg on the River Lech *left* and on to Wies. The Wieskirche *above* is considered to be the finest rococo church in the whole of Europe and was designed and built by Dominikus Zimmerman between 1746 and 1754.

The Romantic Road ends at the mountain resort of Füssen on the River Lech *top right*. A few hundred yards from the Austrian frontier and just outside Füssen the river cascades out of the Alps and over the man-made Lech Falls *above*. Downstream from Füssen is the Forgensee *right*, a man-made reservoir in the midst of the quiet Allgau countryside, and one of the many lakes in the region.

The high walls of the Alps separate Germany from Austria along the southern border of Bavaria and this region, known as the Bavarian Alps, or Upper Bavaria, is a very popular holiday area. Mountains, villages and lakes, such as the Sylvenstein Reservoir *left* and the natural lake at Bayersoien near the winter resort of Garmisch Partenkirchen *bottom left*, provide magnificent scenery. The Hotel Hans Entfeldmühle near Reit im Winkl *right* is an excellent example of a Bavarian Mountain House, and is typical of the area.

The little church of Maria Gern *below* is near Berchtesgaden.

Overleaf: The Benedictine Monastery at Ettal, founded in 1330.

The church at Ramsau *left* and the Sylvenstein in the snow *above* are two typically beautiful Bavarian Alpine scenes.

The Zugspitze *right* stands on the border of Austria and Germany and is the highest peak on German territory. The summit can be reached either by cable car or by funicular railway.

First published in Great Britain 1978 by Colour Libray International Ltd.
© Illustrations CLI/Bruce Coleman Ltd. Colour separations by La Cromolito, Milan, Italy.
Display and text filmsetting by Focus Photoset, London, England.
Printed by Cayfosa and bound by Eurobinder - Barcelona (Spain)
Published by Crescent Books, a división of Crown Publishers Inc.
Library of Congress Catalogue Card No. 77-94419
CRESCENT 1978